CHRIS BUSH

ChatGPT for Programmers

Enhance Your Coding Skills and
Boost Productivity with AI-Powered Assistance
(2024 Guide)

Copyright © 2024 by Chris Bush

All rights reserved. No part of this publication may be reproduced, stored or transmitted in any form or by any means, electronic, mechanical, photocopying, recording, scanning, or otherwise without written permission from the publisher. It is illegal to copy this book, post it to a website, or distribute it by any other means without permission.

First edition

This book was professionally typeset on Reedsy.
Find out more at reedsy.com

Contents

1. Introduction to ChatGPT for Programmers — 1
2. Code Generation with ChatGPT — 3
3. Debugging with ChatGPT — 6
4. Code Review and Quality Assurance — 9
5. Automated Testing with ChatGPT — 13
6. Documentation and Comments — 16
7. Optimization and Performance Tuning — 19
8. ChatGPT for Learning New ProgrammingLanguages — 21
9. Ethical Considerations in AI-Assisted Programming — 24
10. Looking Ahead: ChatGPT and the Future of Programming — 27

1

Introduction to ChatGPT for Programmers

Greetings to the Introduction to ChatGPT for Developers. Within this conversation, we'll delve into the fundamentals of ChatGPT, its relevance in programming, and the ways in which developers can leverage it to improve their tasks.

Comprehending ChatGPT

ChatGPT, crafted by OpenAI, is a sophisticated AI language model. Employing machine learning techniques, it comprehends human language and produces responses that closely resemble human-generated ones. Having undergone extensive pre-training on vast datasets, ChatGPT excels in generating coherent and contextually appropriate responses across various topics and prompts. This versatility enables its application in diverse fields such as natural language processing, text creation, and conversation generation. Built on the Transformer architecture, ChatGPT exhibits high accuracy and efficiency in language-related tasks, contributing to its rising popularity owing to its knack for generating human-like responses across a broad spectrum of inputs.

The Role of AI in Programming

AI plays various roles in the realm of programming. One significant aspect is its ability to automate mundane tasks like debugging, testing, and deployment. Through the utilization of AI algorithms, developers can significantly reduce the time required for testing and deploying software, thus expediting development cycles.

Moreover, AI finds application in programming for tasks such as data analysis and optimization. Machine learning algorithms enable developers to scrutinize extensive datasets, uncovering patterns and trends that might elude human perception. This analytical insight serves to enhance applications and refine user experiences.

Furthermore, AI is instrumental in programming for natural language processing and speech recognition. Developers harness AI algorithms to construct chatbots, virtual assistants, and other conversational interfaces capable of engaging users in a seamless, intuitive manner. This facilitates improved customer interaction and fosters more efficient communication channels.

In essence, AI holds immense potential to transform the programming landscape by streamlining repetitive tasks, refining applications, and crafting more user-friendly interfaces.

2

Code Generation with ChatGPT

Utilizing AI algorithms, ChatGPT streamlines the coding process by automatically generating code based on developers' high-level descriptions. This method enables developers to outline their code needs, prompting the AI to produce the corresponding code.

ChatGPT contributes to code efficiency and effectiveness by aiding in the creation of optimized algorithms. Through inputting datasets and parameters, the AI analyzes the information to generate code tailored to the task at hand.

Moreover, ChatGPT simplifies the creation of boilerplate code by automating its writing. Developers can describe their application, and ChatGPT will produce the foundational code structure, saving time and allowing focus on more intricate programming endeavors.

Additionally, ChatGPT facilitates the development of APIs and libraries by generating code adhering to industry standards and best practices. This promotes the construction of robust and interoperable applications.

In summary, leveraging ChatGPT for code generation significantly diminishes the time and effort required for coding, while simultaneously enhancing code quality and consistency. Nevertheless, developers must meticulously review the AI-generated code to ensure accuracy and alignment with their specific needs.

Writing Code with AI Assistance

Utilizing AI assistance in coding can greatly accelerate the development process and enhance the quality of code. ChatGPT is capable of producing code across various programming languages like Python, JavaScript, and C++.

One method of employing ChatGPT for code creation involves furnishing it with task descriptions or requirements and allowing it to generate code accordingly. For instance, if there's a need to devise a Python function that computes the average of a list of numbers, one can prompt ChatGPT with: "Craft a Python function that accepts a list of numbers and computes their average." ChatGPT will then generate the function's code based on its comprehension of Python syntax and the provided specifications.

Another approach to utilizing ChatGPT for code generation entails presenting it with a snippet of existing code and tasking it to produce analogous code. This proves beneficial in scenarios where repetitive code, such as boilerplate code for a new project, needs to be written. For instance, if there exists Python code that reads data from a CSV file and constructs a list of dictionaries, one can supply this code to ChatGPT and request it to generate similar code for reading data from a different file format, such as JSON. It's imperative to acknowledge that the code produced by ChatGPT may not always be optimal or entirely accurate. As with any AI system, the output from ChatGPT necessitates meticulous review and testing before deployment in production. Moreover, the utilization of AI-generated code raises ethical concerns regarding ownership and originality, which warrant careful consideration.

Producing Boilerplate and Template Code

Boilerplate and template code are snippets of code frequently employed in software development, serving as foundational structures. While boilerplate code is essential but doesn't directly enhance software functionality, template code offers a fundamental framework upon which software can be built.

ChatGPT proves valuable in swiftly generating boilerplate and template code. For instance, by inputting specific parameters and requirements, a programmer can prompt ChatGPT to generate a comprehensive template for the desired code. This feature greatly streamlines the development process, particularly for extensive projects featuring repetitive code segments. Furthermore, ChatGPT's capability to generate code across various programming languages empowers programmers to tackle projects in unfamiliar coding languages.

3

Debugging with ChatGPT

Debugging involves pinpointing and rectifying errors, glitches, and other issues within software code. It's often a demanding and time-consuming endeavor, particularly with intricate software setups. ChatGPT aids in debugging by proposing potential solutions to identified errors. Simply by inputting the error message or problem statement, ChatGPT can offer insights into what might be causing the issue and suggest remedies. Furthermore, it can scrutinize the code and pinpoint potential trouble spots contributing to the error. This capability can significantly streamline the debugging process, especially for complex codebases, saving programmers substantial time and effort. Nevertheless, it's crucial for programmers to validate and test ChatGPT's suggestions to ensure their validity and efficacy. While ChatGPT provides suggestions, they should never be implemented blindly and must undergo thorough analysis and consideration.

AI-driven Bug Identification

Utilizing AI, ChatGPT offers support in recognizing bugs within programming. Employing natural language processing and machine learning methodologies, it conducts an analysis of the code, furnishing suggestions for bug resolution. For instance, it scrutinizes error messages, proposing potential fixes or pinpointing coding structures notorious for inducing bugs.

Furthermore, ChatGPT has the capacity to assimilate knowledge from the code, identifying recurring errors or patterns predisposed to bugs. It can also discern coding methodologies that may precipitate future bugs, enabling programmers to rectify the code preemptively.

In essence, ChatGPT emerges as a valuable asset for debugging and enhancing code quality. Nonetheless, it is imperative to acknowledge that it cannot supplant the proficiency and discernment of programmers. Consequently, any output it generates should undergo meticulous scrutiny and testing.

Proposing Solutions and Enhancements

Certainly, ChatGPT is capable of proposing solutions and enhancements for code. One method it employs is utilizing machine learning algorithms to scrutinize extensive code datasets, recognizing recurring patterns and typical mistakes. Drawing from this examination, it can recommend alterations to the code that are likely to yield positive results. Furthermore, it can refine its suggestions by learning from the adjustments made by developers.

Alternatively, it can utilize natural language processing techniques to evaluate code documentation and offer recommendations for enhancing code readability and manageability. This may encompass suggestions regarding naming conventions, comments, and formatting.

In essence, ChatGPT holds promise in aiding programmers in pinpointing and rectifying bugs, enhancing code quality, and boosting productivity. Nonetheless, it's essential to emphasize that its suggestions should undergo review and validation by human programmers, as they may not always be precise or suitable for the specific context.

4

Code Review and Quality Assurance

Ensuring the efficiency, security, and reliability of code is crucial in software development, which is why code review and quality assurance play vital roles. AI offers valuable assistance to programmers in these areas, aiding in error detection, code enhancement, and adherence to industry standards. Here's how ChatGPT can support programmers in code review and quality assurance:

1. Automated code review: ChatGPT conducts automated code reviews to pinpoint errors, vulnerabilities, and potential issues, including syntax errors, style violations, and adherence to best practices.
2. Code optimization: ChatGPT suggests optimization techniques to boost performance, reduce resource usage, and enhance efficiency. It also recommends refactoring strategies to enhance modularity, maintainability, and scalability.
3. Test case generation: ChatGPT creates test cases to validate code functionality and uncover potential issues, including edge cases and overlooked scenarios.
4. Security analysis: ChatGPT aids in security analysis by identifying vulnerabilities and proposing solutions. It performs static code analysis to detect security risks and promotes adherence to security best practices.

5. Code documentation: ChatGPT assists in generating comprehensive code documentation for functions, classes, and modules, making the code more understandable and maintainable.

Leveraging AI for code review and quality assurance streamlines the process, reducing manual effort, improving code quality, and enhancing overall development efficiency.

Utilizing ChatGPT for Code Evaluation

Employing ChatGPT for code evaluation involves examining the code and suggesting enhancements based on established best practices and standards. Here are various ways in which ChatGPT can contribute to code evaluation:

1. Enhancing code style: ChatGPT offers insights into code style by evaluating aspects like code indentation, formatting, naming conventions, and documentation, thereby suggesting improvements.
2. Improving code quality: ChatGPT aids in enhancing code quality by identifying potential bugs, inefficiencies, and security vulnerabilities, thus suggesting enhancements for better performance.
3. Automating code review: ChatGPT streamlines the code review process by automatically analyzing code against existing guidelines and standards, reducing the time and effort required for manual review.
4. Facilitating code review collaboration: ChatGPT fosters collaboration among developers by providing a platform for sharing and reviewing code changes. It enables developers to provide feedback and collaborate on enhancing code quality.

In essence, ChatGPT serves as a valuable tool for enhancing code quality and simplifying the code evaluation process in software development.

CODE REVIEW AND QUALITY ASSURANCE

Ensuring Code Quality with AI

Leveraging Artificial Intelligence (AI) is instrumental in enhancing the quality of code by pinpointing potential issues prior to deployment. AI-driven tools possess the capability to scrutinize code comprehensively, detecting errors, security loopholes, performance bottlenecks, and more. Detecting these issues at an early stage empowers developers to rectify them proactively, thereby averting any disruptions for end-users.

There are several ways in which AI, like ChatGPT, can contribute to code review and quality assurance:

1. Automated code reviews: AI-driven tools conduct thorough analyses of code, furnishing feedback on various aspects such as syntax errors, adherence to coding conventions, and security vulnerabilities.
2. Predictive analytics: AI aids in recognizing patterns and foreseeing potential pitfalls in code, allowing developers to preemptively address issues before they impact users.
3. Code optimization: AI assists in optimizing code for better performance, efficient memory usage, and other relevant factors, thereby elevating the overall quality of the codebase.
4. Test automation: AI-powered tools automate the testing process, expediting it and enhancing accuracy, ensuring that the code functions as intended.
5. Code suggestions: AI offers suggestions for code snippets and assists with code completion, expediting the development process and ensuring code accuracy and reliability.

In summary, harnessing ChatGPT for code review and quality assurance endeavors can significantly elevate the standard of code, streamline development timelines, and enrich user experiences.

5

Automated Testing with ChatGPT

Automated testing involves using software tools to examine software or applications, ensuring they function as intended and meet requirements. ChatGPT can automate this process by crafting test cases and scripts. It evaluates code to pinpoint potential bugs and can generate test cases covering various scenarios and edge cases for comprehensive testing. Moreover, ChatGPT can automate test case execution, minimizing manual intervention and enhancing efficiency, thereby expediting the testing process. Overall, ChatGPT serves as a beneficial asset in software testing, enhancing software quality and mitigating the likelihood of errors and bugs.

Writing Test Cases with AI Assistance

Utilizing AI can aid programmers in crafting test cases for software applications, which are crucial for verifying functional requirements and pinpointing any flaws. ChatGPT offers support by proposing inputs and anticipated outputs for various functions or methods, as well as assisting in generating comprehensive test data to cover diverse input scenarios.

Through code analysis, ChatGPT can suggest testing strategies for different code segments and highlight potential edge cases necessitating extra scrutiny. Furthermore, it can streamline the creation of automated test scripts, enabling repetitive testing and maintaining consistent results.

Leveraging ChatGPT for test case formulation and automated testing allows programmers to streamline their workflow, saving time and effort in both crafting and executing test cases, all the while upholding the software application's quality.

Automating Test Execution and Reporting

Utilizing ChatGPT for automating test execution and reporting streamlines the testing process. Test automation involves employing software tools to oversee test execution and compare actual outcomes with expected ones, aiming to maintain the software's quality standards—a pivotal phase in software development.

With ChatGPT, automating test execution involves generating test cases according to requirements and specifications. These cases can be automatically produced, leveraging ChatGPT's ability to discern patterns and generate test cases from input data. Such automation significantly reduces the time and effort typically required for manual test case generation.

Furthermore, ChatGPT facilitates test reporting, encompassing the documentation and communication of test results. This entails generating reports that summarize test outcomes, pinpoint issues, and suggest improvements. Leveraging ChatGPT for test reporting automates this process, saving time and enhancing accuracy. Trained to analyze test results, ChatGPT can identify issues and generate reports summarizing results along with improvement recommendations. This capability enables organizations to promptly and efficiently address issues, ultimately enhancing the software product's overall quality.

6

Documentation and Comments

Programming relies heavily on documentation and comments, crucial for developers to comprehend and uphold code. Documentation elucidates the code's functionality, purpose, and usage, while comments expound on its logic and furnish context. AI offers assistance in both these areas.

AI aids in documentation by automatically crafting explanations based on the code. Through natural language processing, models scrutinize the code and produce documentation detailing its purpose, input parameters, return values, and usage. This automation saves developers time and ensures thorough documentation.

Moreover, AI contributes to commenting by analyzing code and generating explanations of its logic. This proves invaluable for intricate algorithms or cryptic code. AI-generated comments supply context and enhance readability, facilitating code comprehension and maintenance.

Nevertheless, it's crucial to recognize that AI-generated comments and documentation might lack accuracy or completeness. Developers must scrutinize and validate the generated content to ensure correctness and sufficiency. Additionally, developers should continue to craft their own documentation and comments to offer supplementary context and insights.

Generating Code Documentation with ChatGPT

Utilizing ChatGPT for coding purposes extends to the creation of code documentation, which is a valuable application. Documentation plays a crucial role in software development by facilitating comprehension of program functionalities and usage for other developers. Through ChatGPT, coders can automate the generation of code documentation, thereby saving valuable time and effort.

ChatGPT functions by analyzing the code and producing descriptive comments elucidating the purpose and behavior of the code. It can also craft documentation for various elements such as classes, functions, and variables, offering insights into their input and output parameters. Automating documentation generation ensures that code remains well-documented and easier to manage, even in scenarios where manual documentation authoring may be impractical due to constraints on time or resources.

Moreover, ChatGPT extends its utility to aiding in the creation of code comments, which serve to explain the functionality of specific code segments or provide contextual information for fellow developers collaborating on the codebase. By analyzing the code, ChatGPT can generate comments detailing how the code operates, its functionality, and the rationale behind its inclusion.

In summary, leveraging ChatGPT for code documentation and commenting endeavors enhances code quality and fosters improved accessibility for other developers.

Writing Effective Comments and Doc strings

Crafting effective comments and doc strings plays a pivotal role in programming, aiding in code comprehension for fellow developers and streamlining maintenance and debugging processes. Here's how ChatGPT can be instrumental in this domain:

1. Crafting clear and succinct comments: Utilize ChatGPT to generate articulate comments that elucidate the functionality of your code. Simply furnish ChatGPT with a brief overview of the code, and it can formulate a comment that precisely outlines its purpose.
2. Automating doc string creation: Doc strings are indispensable in Python programming, delineating a function's operation and its parameters. ChatGPT can automate doc string generation by analyzing the function's inputs and outputs.
3. Documenting code flow: Clarifying the code's logic and flow can sometimes pose a challenge. In such instances, ChatGPT can aid in generating comments that expound on the code's rationale and its progression.
4. Generating inline comments: Harness ChatGPT to produce inline comments elucidating specific lines or blocks of code. This feature proves particularly beneficial when navigating extensive codebases or collaborating with other developers.
5. Ensuring grammar and spelling accuracy: ChatGPT can also lend assistance in scrutinizing the grammar and spelling of your comments and doc strings, ensuring their lucidity and correctness.

In essence, ChatGPT serves as a valuable tool for generating coherent and precise comments, crafting doc strings, documenting code flow, generating inline comments, and verifying grammar and spelling accuracy.

7

Optimization and Performance Tuning

Enhancing efficiency and refining performance play pivotal roles in software development. Crafting code that runs smoothly is imperative for the triumph of any application, be it desktop-based, web-oriented, or mobile-centric. Utilizing AI proves beneficial in streamlining and enhancing performance by scrutinizing code and pinpointing areas ripe for enhancement.

ChatGPT offers assistance in fine-tuning and optimizing performance through code analysis and provision of improvement suggestions. For instance, it can pinpoint inefficient segments of code and propose optimizations. Moreover, it can recommend alterations to algorithms or data structures to potentially boost performance.

Another area where ChatGPT proves valuable is in memory management, a crucial facet of performance optimization. It scrutinizes code to identify opportunities for reducing memory usage, such as through object reuse or downsizing data structures.

In summary, ChatGPT aids in optimization and performance tuning by furnishing developers with insights and recommendations to bolster the efficiency of their code.

Using AI to Identify Performance Bottlenecks

Artificial intelligence (AI) has the capability to pinpoint performance bottlenecks within code by scrutinizing its execution patterns and pinpointing sections of code that are experiencing prolonged execution times compared to others. For instance, AI can analyze the duration of execution for various functions within a program and highlight those consuming the most time. Once these bottlenecks are recognized, developers can enhance the code to boost its performance.

Moreover, AI can offer assistance in performance optimization by proposing alterations to the code that could enhance its efficiency. This could involve suggesting adjustments to algorithms, data structures, or coding methodologies that might enhance performance. Furthermore, AI can aid in fine-tuning system parameters like memory allocation, thread management, and network configurations to optimize overall system performance.

Proposing Enhancement Tactics

ChatGPT is capable of proposing enhancement tactics aimed at refining code performance. One aspect involves scrutinizing the code to pinpoint inefficient algorithms or data structures responsible for performance bottlenecks. Furthermore, it can offer suggestions for parallelizing the code or refining memory usage to enhance execution speed. Additionally, ChatGPT can advise on tailoring code for particular hardware or platforms, like leveraging vectorization or GPU acceleration. In essence, ChatGPT emerges as a beneficial resource for programmers seeking to enhance their code's efficiency.

8

ChatGPT for Learning New ProgrammingLanguages

Utilizing ChatGPT as a tool for grasping new programming languages offers several advantages:

1. Code Translation: ChatGPT excels in translating code from one programming language to another. This feature proves invaluable for learners as it provides insight into how code is structured and written across different languages.
2. Provision of Examples and Tutorials: ChatGPT is adept at generating comprehensive examples and tutorials tailored to various programming languages. These resources aid learners in comprehending the syntax and organization of unfamiliar languages.
3. Debugging Assistance: ChatGPT serves as a helpful companion in identifying and rectifying errors within code written in a new programming language. By inputting code, users can receive suggestions for troubleshooting and resolving issues.
4. Idea Generation for Projects: ChatGPT can propose innovative project ideas suited to a new programming language.

>   This feature facilitates hands-on practice and implementation of acquired knowledge.
> 5. Q&A Support: Users can pose questions regarding a new programming language to ChatGPT, which promptly provides informative responses. This interaction aids in grasping fundamental concepts and principles of the language.

In essence, ChatGPT emerges as a valuable asset for learning new programming languages, offering assistance in code translation, example generation, debugging, project ideation, and question answering.

Utilizing ChatGPT as an Educational Tool

In the realm of programming, ChatGPT serves as a valuable resource for acquiring knowledge about different programming languages. By posing inquiries related to syntax, data structures, and programming principles, programmers can leverage ChatGPT to gain insights. Through explanations and code examples, ChatGPT facilitates comprehension and application of novel concepts. Moreover, it can offer recommendations on various learning materials like online tutorials, documentation, and books. ChatGPT is adept at suggesting practice exercises and challenges to enhance proficiency in a new programming language. Furthermore, it provides assistance in troubleshooting common errors and challenges encountered during the learning process.

Translating Code Between Different Languages

Converting code from one programming language to another can be facilitated with the help of ChatGPT. This process utilizes natural language processing to transform code written in one language into textual format, then generates corresponding code in the desired programming language. Although this method may not yield flawless translations every time, it offers considerable time and effort savings compared to manually rewriting the code. Additionally, it aids programmers in swiftly mastering new programming languages by offering an automated means to translate familiar code into a new language.

9

Ethical Considerations in AI-Assisted Programming

When employing AI in programming, ethical considerations must be carefully weighed. Here are several crucial issues to ponder:

1. Bias: Like any other machine learning tool, ChatGPT might carry biases inherited from its training data. Programmers should acknowledge this bias and work to minimize its influence.
2. Accountability: Assigning responsibility for decisions made by AI in programming can be challenging. Programmers must accept accountability for the outcomes generated by the AI they utilize.
3. Privacy: To operate effectively, ChatGPT may necessitate access to sensitive data. Programmers must prioritize safeguarding user privacy and ensuring secure storage of any collected data.
4. Transparency: The utilization of AI in programming can obscure the decision-making process. Programmers should strive for transparency in the AI they employ, enabling a clear understanding of decision rationale.
5. Job Displacement: The advancement of AI may lead to

job displacement within the programming sector. Programmers should recognize this potential impact and take proactive measures to address it.

Responsible Use of AI in Coding

Using AI in coding responsibly means understanding the potential outcomes and taking measures to mitigate negative effects. It's crucial to use AI to augment human decision-making rather than replacing it entirely. Recognizing and addressing biases in AI systems is also important. Developers should be open about their AI usage, including the data used for training, and seek consent from users when necessary. Moreover, they should adhere to any legal or regulatory guidelines relevant to AI in coding to ensure compliance.

Tackling Prejudice and Equity in Artificial Intelligence Instruments

Ensuring fairness and addressing bias in AI tools is crucial to prevent discrimination against any specific group or community. Bias can creep into AI tools through the data used for training, the algorithms employed, or the tool's design.

To tackle these issues, diverse and representative datasets should be utilized for training AI tools. Rigorous data cleaning and preprocessing must be conducted to eliminate any inherent biases. Additionally, it's vital to ensure that the algorithms employed do not introduce biases during data processing.

To verify the fairness and impartiality of AI tools, they should undergo testing using varied and representative datasets to detect and rectify any biases. The outcomes of these tools should be evaluated for fairness, and any identified biases should be addressed.

Involving individuals from diverse backgrounds in the design and development of AI tools is also essential. This inclusive approach helps prevent unintentional bias from seeping into the tool during its creation.

In essence, a dedication to fairness and equity is paramount in the development and utilization of AI tools to ensure they benefit everyone equitably.

10

Looking Ahead: ChatGPT and the Future of Programming

Looking ahead, the landscape of programming with AI and ChatGPT appears promising and brimming with opportunities. These AI-driven tools have already transformed how we approach writing, debugging, and refining code. Looking forward, we anticipate the emergence of even more sophisticated AI systems capable of delving deeper into code, recognizing patterns, and proposing intricate and refined solutions. Moreover, AI holds the potential to democratize programming by making it more accessible to individuals without extensive expertise, thus expanding the pool of people proficient in programming languages for everyday applications. Furthermore, AI can play a crucial role in bolstering code security and safeguarding privacy, thereby mitigating the risks associated with hacking and data breaches. Nonetheless, it remains imperative to conscientiously address ethical considerations and uphold responsible practices in the utilization of AI in programming to prevent adverse repercussions.

Contemporary Patterns and Anticipated Projections

Emerging trends indicate an increasing adoption of AI-supported programming within the industry. Numerous tools and platforms are being devised to aid developers in various aspects of code creation, testing, and upkeep. As AI capabilities progress, these tools are expected to become more sophisticated, adept at tackling complex tasks.

Looking ahead, there's a potential for AI systems like ChatGPT to take on the role of generating entire software applications, streamlining much of the development process. However, it's crucial to address the ethical considerations inherent in such a scenario, particularly concerning the potential impact on employment within the software development sector.

In summary, the future landscape of programming likely entails a collaboration between human expertise and machine intelligence, aimed at crafting software that's more efficient, dependable, and impactful. Consequently, programmers should embrace these evolving technologies and seek ways to integrate them into their practices responsibly and ethically.

Getting ready for a Programming Environment Dominated by Artificial Intelligence

Getting ready for a programming landscape influenced by AI requires programmers to keep abreast of the latest advancements in the field. This entails familiarizing themselves with new AI tools and methodologies, while also being mindful of ethical considerations and the responsible application of AI in programming.

To prepare for this AI-centric programming environment, professionals should engage in continuous learning and skill development. This could involve attending industry events, taking online courses, and networking with peers and experts in the domain.

Moreover, maintaining proficiency in fundamental programming skills such as algorithmic design, data structures, and software engineering principles remains crucial. While AI technologies can streamline various aspects of programming, they can't replace the need for a solid grasp of these foundational concepts.

Lastly, programmers need to acknowledge the potential impact of AI on the job market and the future of work. While AI might automate certain tasks, there will always be a demand for skilled programmers capable of designing, implementing, and maintaining AI systems. By staying informed and adaptable, programmers can position themselves for success in an AI-driven future.

Here are some excellent prompts tailored for programmers:

Follow this prompt precisely as it's presented below in GPT Chat. Then, experiment with altering the terms enclosed in quotation marks to suit your preferences. This prompt is especially beneficial for programmers, serving as a potent tool for your use.

Prompt:
   You will assume the role of a programmer and write code in "Python" to develop an application focusing on "environmental pollution". The application's purpose will be to "depict Environmental Pollution in Europe for each country".

You will take on the role of a programmer and craft code in "HTML" to create a static website centered on "environmental pollution". The website's aim will be to "showcase Environmental Pollution in Europe for each country".

You're an experienced programmer with over 20 years of expertise and will approach tasks accordingly. Debug the following code: [Copy and paste the code here and remove the quotes.]

www.ingramcontent.com/pod-product-compliance
Lightning Source LLC
LaVergne TN
LVHW021050100526
838202LV00082B/5418